Chanté

Words of Wisdom

Walking the Straight Path through Proverbs

Lifeway Press®
Brentwood, Tennessee

© 2023 Lifeway Press®

No part of this work may be reproduced or transmitted in any form or by any means, electronic or mechanical, including photocopying and recording, or by any information storage or retrieval system, except as may be expressly permitted in writing by the publisher. Requests for permission should be addressed in writing to Lifeway Press®; 200 Powell Place, Suite 100; Brentwood, TN, 37027.

ISBN 978-1-0877-6742-0
Item 005838147
Dewey Decimal Classification Number: 242
Subject Heading: DEVOTIONAL LITERATURE / BIBLE STUDY AND TEACHING / GOD

Printed in the United States of America

Student Ministry Publishing
Lifeway Resources
200 Powell Place, Suite 100
Brentwood, TN, 37027-7707

We believe that the Bible has God for its author; salvation for its end; and truth, without any mixture of error, for its matter and that all Scripture is totally true and trustworthy. To review Lifeway's doctrinal guideline, please visit www.lifeway.com/doctrinalguideline.

Unless otherwise noted, all Scripture quotations are taken from the Christian Standard Bible®, Copyright © 2017 by Holman Bible Publishers. Used by permission. Christian Standard Bible® and CSB® are federally registered trademarks of Holman Bible Publishers.

publishing team

Director, Student Ministry
Ben Trueblood

Manager, Student Ministry Publishing
John Paul Basham

Editorial Team Leader
Karen Daniel

Writer
Jennifer Dixon

Content Editor
Kyle Wiltshire

Production Editors
April-Lyn Caouette
Stephanie Cross

Graphic Designer
Shiloh Stufflebeam

TABLE OF CONTENTS

04
intro

05
getting started

06
wisdom vs. foolishness

36
the wisdom of Solomon

84
wisdom that endures

106
W-I-S-D-O-M

Intro

Promises are not ifs, ands, or buts. They are sure and solid, ironclad. No circumstances can change their certainty. Promises like Jesus's words in Matthew 28:20—"I am with you always, to the end of the age"—and Paul's words in Romans 10:9—"If you confess with your mouth, 'Jesus is Lord,' and believe in your heart that God raised him from the dead, you will be saved"—can be found throughout the Bible.

However, there is a difference between a promise and a principle. While biblical promises are certain, principles are not. For example, 2 Corinthians 9:6 says, "The person who sows sparingly will also reap sparingly, and the person who sows generously will also reap generously." This is an image from farming. If a farmer plants only a few seeds, he won't have many crops when it comes time to harvest. If the farmer plants a lot of seeds, he will have an abundance of crops when it comes time to harvest.

The difference between a principle and a promise is that circumstances can interfere with the certainty of a principle. If a farmer plants a lot of seeds and a huge flood comes the next day and washes them away, he won't reap a gigantic harvest as the principle states. However, most of the time this doesn't happen. So the principle is sound, even if circumstances can alter its certainty from time to time.

The book of Proverbs is filled with promises and principles, but it's important to know the difference between the two. For example, Proverbs 16:3 says, "Commit your activities to the LORD, and your plans will be established." The principle is this: giving your plans and future to God is better than not giving Him your plans and future. It doesn't mean that if you give your activities to God, He is bound to bless them and establish everything you want.

Ultimately, the book of Proverbs is filled with great wisdom. When we obey the wisdom of God's Word, He helps us, comes alongside us, and comforts us as we journey through life. That is a promise!

Getting Started

*This devotional contains thirty days of content, broken down into sections. Each day is divided into three elements—**discover, delight,** and **display**—to help you grow in your faith.*

discover

This section helps you examine the passage in light of who God is and determine what it says about your identity in relationship to Him. Included here is the daily Scripture reading and key verses, along with illustrations and commentary to guide you as you learn more about God's Word.

delight

In this section, you'll be challenged by questions and activities that help you see how God is alive and active in every detail of His Word and your life.

display

Here's where you take action. This section calls you to apply what you've learned through each day.

Each day also includes a prayer activity at the conclusion of the devotion.

Throughout the devotional, you'll also find extra items to help you connect with the topic personally, such as Scripture memory verses and interactive articles.

Words of Wisdom

Wisdom vs. Foolishness

SECTION 1

If someone asked you if you wanted to be wise or foolish, you would undoubtedly choose to be wise. However, when life presents us with opportunities to choose between the two, we often choose foolishness. We do this when we listen to the wrong voices, ignore God's Word, or follow our own paths. In Proverbs 1–9, Solomon reveals helpful ways we can choose wisdom and avoid the call of foolishness.

DAY 1

Where Wisdom Begins

discover

READ PROVERBS 1.

**The fear of the LORD is the beginning of knowledge;
fools despise wisdom and discipline.
— Proverbs 1:7**

As you read Proverbs, you will be presented with a choice: follow wisdom or ignore it. While the right answer might seem obvious at first glance, it is important to acknowledge that there are likely a lot of big questions swirling around in your mind: Who am I? What will I do in the future? What do I want to accomplish? What will my life look like when I'm older? Not knowing the answers to these questions can be stressful. However, before you try to answer them, you must decide to seek wisdom. Refusing to do so only leads to foolishness.

Proverbs 1 tells us that there will be many voices calling for our attention. There are voices that will call us to use others for our own gain, to not listen to reason, and to be lazy about life in general. It's tough to discern whether a voice is leading us toward a better future or toward our own downfall. Wisdom will be the key to knowing which voices to follow and which to ignore.

So where does a person get wisdom? It begins with the fear of the Lord. If we believe God exists and created this world and everything in it (including us) and that He is involved in this world (including our lives), then the next step is to fear Him. This means to honor and respect Him and regard Him with awe. This belief in God's existence and presence is where your wisdom will begin. Believe God is present during all your life—caring for you, watching over you, wanting to help you, and being ready to lead you back to Him when you've gone astray—and wisdom will follow.

delight

What path do you see yourself on right now—the path of wisdom or foolishness? Why do you see yourself on this path?

What do you believe the Bible means when it says to "fear God"? Compare those thoughts with being afraid of something. How are they alike and how are they different?

display

Which voice has the most influence in your life? Below, write out a sentence explaining why this voice has so much influence over you. Is it healthy for that voice to have so much influence in your life?

To fear God means to treat Him with respect, awe, and worship but also acknowledge He has the power to change your life in an instant. He should be top priority in all your decision making, and yes, God can be terrifying in the sense that He can wipe out the world with just a word. However, He cares for you. The Bible says "The LORD is compassionate and gracious, slow to anger and abounding in faithful love" (Ps. 103:8). He is a voice of influence that has your best interests at heart.

Thank God that He has your best interests at heart. Ask Him to help you listen for His wisdom when it is presented to you. Talk to Him about your own struggle to find wisdom or to avoid foolishness. Commit to Him that you will consider Him in your daily life decisions.

DAY 2

Wisdom Is for the Taking

discover

READ PROVERBS 2.

> **For the LORD gives wisdom; from his mouth come knowledge and understanding.**
> **— Proverbs 2:6**

Imagine the thing you want more than anything else in the world. What would you do to get it? How hard would you work for it? How much would you give up in order to have it? The sacrifice to go after the thing you want most in the world is how the father in Proverbs instructs his son to go after wisdom. He compares searching for a treasure to going after wisdom; but where is the son to find wisdom?

Remember from Proverbs 1, wisdom is compared to a woman calling out in public places for people to come listen. Wisdom is actually not hidden but is being given out right now. The difficult part is knowing which information being given out is wise or foolish. Proverbs 2:6 says that "the LORD gives wisdom" and James 1:5 instructs "Now if any of you lacks wisdom, he should ask God—who gives to all generously and ungrudgingly—and it will be given to him." So, to start receiving wisdom, we need to first ask God for it. This may seem simplistic, but this step in our wisdom journey cannot be underestimated.

We will need a direct line to God if we want to be wise. There is no way around it. Do you want to know how to get a direct line to God? It's through Jesus. God doesn't wait for you to make the first move— He already made it. He sent Jesus to be our connection to Him. All you need to do is get to know Him. Learn about His life. Practice His teachings. Ask questions about Him from others you respect. Your journey to wisdom begins with your journey to knowing Jesus, and ultimately, God the Father.

delight

Where do you go when you want to learn God's wisdom? List the sources you believe wisdom can come from.

List three habits that will be easy for you to maintain so that you can continue getting connected with Jesus. (Tip: Committing to continue this book can be one of those habits.)

display

Wisdom comes from God, and God makes Himself known to us through Jesus. Do you know Jesus? Give a thoughtful evaluation of where your relationship with Him is, then decide what the next step is for you to get to know Him more. Do you know nothing about Him? Then maybe your first step is to find a church community to help you learn. Already a part of a church? Maybe your next step is to start asking questions to learn more or to ask to be discipled by an older Christian. Think through your relationship and decide on your next move.

Ask God to make you want wisdom more than anything. Thank Him that He sent Jesus to show how much He wants a relationship with you. Lastly, ask God how you can know Him more. In what ways are you not connecting with Him in your everyday life?

DAY 3

Trust in the Lord

discover

READ PROVERBS 3.

Trust in the Lord with all your heart, and do not rely on your own understanding; in all your ways know him, and he will make your paths straight.
— Proverbs 3:5-6

Are you familiar with the word "psychosomatic"? It's a big word that simply means your mind and your body are connected. In other words, your thoughts impact your body. Have you ever started sweating profusely when you were nervous? Or do you ever crave food when you are stressed? Do you ever get a burst of energy when a great idea pops in your head? All these experiences are evidence that your thoughts have a direct impact on your body. Here in Proverbs 3, Solomon said trusting in the Lord will be healing for your body.

Trust in God is taking Him at His word, and believing what He says is true. God says a lot to His people throughout the Bible, but three truths that will be beneficial for you to build your trust in Him are: God loves you, God wants good for you, and God can handle anything. These truths can calm anxious thoughts, heal broken hearts, and give hope in a time when it feels hopeless.

Solomon also said to "not rely on your own understanding." He isn't saying you can't know anything for yourself; he's saying you don't know everything. There are always things happening and viewpoints you can't grasp but God can. Trust He is in control and talk to Him when you feel out of control. This way of going through life will benefit you spiritually and physically.

delight

Look up the following verses. How does each one support the truth listed next to it?

John 3:16 – God loves you.

Romans 8:28-34 – God wants good for you.

Hebrews 1:1-4 – God can handle anything.

How can you use these truths in your everyday life to give you peace and confidence?

display

Think through a situation you are facing right now that is causing you to panic, worry, or stress. How can the truths about God help you face this situation? The feelings of uneasiness may not go away completely, but it is always a good idea to talk to God about how you are feeling and what problems you are facing. Cling to His truth as a guide to help you respond in those troubling times.

Tell God about what gives you inner joy and what troubles your soul. Hold Him to His Word. Tell Him about how you want the things He has promised in His Word. Confess times when you haven't trusted Him and ask Him to build your trust.

DAY 4

Avoid the Wicked

discover

READ PROVERBS 4.

Keep off the path of the wicked; don't proceed on the way of evil ones.
— Proverbs 4:14

It is usually easy to tell who the "bad guy" is when watching a movie. Screenwriters and directors let the audience in on who is planning evil and who is fighting good. But sometimes a movie gives a good plot twist, and someone who seemed to be good is actually working for evil. In today's passage Solomon warned his son to "keep off the path of the wicked" and said "don't proceed on the way of evil ones." How as Christ followers are we to find out which way is wicked and which is not?

There are clues in Proverbs that help us determine the way of the wicked. That way you will know what path not to follow. The wicked want to attack innocent people for fun (see Prov. 1:11). They take from others for their own gain (see Prov. 1:13). They make plans to harm others and accuse innocent people of wrong doing (see Prov. 3:29-30). They want to see others mess up (see Prov. 4:16). To sum up all the clues given: the wicked want to hurt others.

This hurtful spirit is not the way of wisdom, and it is definitely not God's way. To take others down out of spite, jealousy, envy, or revenge is not the way God works. Remember God loves all that He has made (see Ps. 145:8-9). God's work is about healing, restoration, service, and community. Avoid the way of the wicked when you see it in others and when you see it in yourself.

delight

Look up these passages. In each one, someone caused harm to an innocent person: Genesis 4:6-12; 2 Samuel 11:14-17; 12:7-12; 1 Kings 21:1-24. How did God respond to their wicked actions? What can you learn about God's stance on hurting others for our own gain?

Have you seen wickedness in others or yourself? What can you do to avoid its allure, or what have you done in the past to avoid it?

display

The desire to hurt others resides in even the most righteous people. David was considered a man after God's own heart, but God wouldn't stand for even David, His beloved, to harm an innocent person (see 2 Sam. 12:1-12). It's important to be aware of your own tendencies to hurt others. It usually begins with thoughts of jealousy, envy, discontentment, or fear. Be on alert for those thoughts. Name them for what they are and seek solace in what is good, true, and life-giving.

Tell God any struggles you have resisting wickedness. Ask Him to fix your mind on what is good, true, and life-giving. If you feel that influences in your life are drawing you toward wickedness, ask God to bring you a community of people who will support you as you seek wisdom.

DAY 5

Consider the Outcome

discover

READ PROVERBS 5.

For a man's ways are before the LORD**'s eyes, and he considers all his paths. A wicked man's iniquities will trap him; he will become tangled in the ropes of his own sin.**
— Proverbs 5:21-22

Have you ever started a project, a sport, a club, or even a relationship, only to find that you didn't think through the consequences of taking on this new commitment in your life? Maybe you didn't ask yourself enough questions before saying yes or you made assumptions about what it would be like, only to find out the reality was much different. In Proverbs 5, Solomon encouraged his son to consider the outcome of his decisions.

Solomon warned his son not to follow the forbidden woman. He told him that her words were enticing, but in the end following her would be devastating. His best years would be given to someone who did not reciprocate his love. She would take from him, and in the end, his physical and emotional health would be spent (see vv. 9-11). The alternative to this life is staying the course God has for him.

Solomon said if you stay the course of following God, He will watch over you. God knows all the outcomes of each decision you will make. If you will discipline yourself to seek Him, the final outcome will be beneficial for you. As Romans 10:11 says, "Everyone who believes on [God] will not be put to shame." No one knows exactly what his or her life will look like five, ten, or twenty years down the road, but if you follow God you won't be disappointed at the end of your life.

delight

In what ways do you consider God when making decisions? Do you acknowledge His instructions to you or do you ignore them?

What would more discipline in following God look like for you? What are areas of your life where you think you could apply more discipline to achieve the beneficial life God promises?

display

You probably are bombarded daily with pictures, ads, and stories that tell you someone else's life is better than yours. It's a temptation you will most likely face every day of your life—to choose the work God has given you to do or to desire someone else's situation. In those moments, think of the outcome: If I seek what they have, where will I end up emotionally, physically, spiritually, and relationally? Just remember no one loves you, cares for you, and wants what is best for you more than God. Trust that He knows what He is doing with you.

Talk to God about times when you have been enticed into neglecting His way and end up following someone else's instead. Tell Him about the things you desire. Thank Him that He ultimately wants to give you what your heart needs most (see Ps. 37:4). Ask Him to help you come up with ideas about how to discipline yourself to follow Him.

Memory Verse

Trust in the LORD with all your heart, and do not rely on your own understanding; in all your ways know him, and he will make your paths straight.

— Proverbs 3:5-6

DAY 6

Striving for Unity

discover

READ PROVERBS 6.

The LORD hates six things; in fact, seven are detestable to him: arrogant eyes, a lying tongue, hands that shed innocent blood, a heart that plots wicked schemes, feet eager to run to evil, a lying witness who gives false testimony, and one who stirs up trouble among brothers.
— Proverbs 6:16-19

Do you know your family members' pet peeves? How about one of your teachers'? Do you notice what really makes them angry? Do you know just how to push someone else's button? Proverbs 6:16-19 lays out what upsets God. These are not merely annoyances like pet peeves but really upset Him. When we do these things, they compete with His desires for us.

God hates the things listed in verses 16-19. "Hates" is a strong word. It would be foolish to take on any of these behaviors if God clearly states His enormous distaste for them. Notice how in verse 16, Solomon draws attention to a seventh thing that rounds out the list of behaviors God hates: "One who stirs up trouble among brothers." This seventh item summarizes why all the other six things make God upset. He desires unity that works for good among His people. Those who want to stir up trouble are setting themselves against what God wants.

God wants you to be in community with others—loving them, encouraging them, and serving them like Jesus would. He also wants you to receive love, encouragement, and the feeling of Jesus's presence from others. When you take on any of the behaviors listed in verses 16-19, you prevent the flow of God's love from reaching the very people He wants His love given to.

delight

Read Jesus's prayer in John 17:20-26. What does Jesus want most for those who believe in Him? How would the seven things listed in Proverbs 6 be opposed to what Jesus wants for His people?

Look over the list of seven things God hates. Do you see any of these behaviors in yourself? If so, how can you eliminate them from your life?

display

Take time to think through your friends. Who supports you in your faith? Who builds you up? Also take time to consider who might be stirring up trouble. What boundaries might you need to consider setting? Now, consider your own behaviors. Do you stir up trouble to separate others? How can you work toward unity? Journal all your thoughts. Think about talking to your student ministry leader about how you can bring unity among your group.

Ask God to bring you friends who encourage you and to help you set boundaries among people who don't. Confess times you stirred up trouble among others. Talk to God about what He desires for the relationships in your life.

DAY 7

Tune Out

discover

READ PROVERBS 7.

**Don't let your heart turn aside to her
ways; don't stray onto her paths.
— Proverbs 7:25**

Have you ever used a photo editing app to give the illusion of perfection in your pictures? Have you ever looked at how others change their photos to make themselves look more attractive? People will create the illusion of freedom, satisfaction, and fun to entice others to follow them. In Proverbs 7, a wicked woman went to extreme lengths to make a man her admirer. She dressed seductively. She sprayed her bed with perfumes. She laid out a plan for the two of them to be together without being caught. She made everything sound as if their sin would be wonderful. She wanted to use him for her own pleasure but had no intention of doing what was best for him.

The father warned his sons not to let their hearts turn aside to her ways. He knew the outcome would lead to destruction. He had seen countless men suffer from following this woman when they gave in to her advances. Her persistent pleading and flattering talk were convincing.

If you have to be talked into something you feel is wrong, it's probably a sign that you should run from it. When you allow the voices of those who want to lead you astray to keep talking, you will eventually falter. If you have to listen to these voices in secret because you know a good friend would tell you, "This is not a good idea," that's a sign you shouldn't be listening. Wisdom tells us we must not go along with those who don't love and care for us as God does.

delight

Have you ever allowed someone to talk you into something you felt was wrong? What happened and what can you do to keep it from happening again? (Don't beat yourself up about it, but try to think objectively about what you could do differently in the future.)

Look up the following verses. How can they serve as reminders that God wants what is best for you?

John 3:16-17:

1 John 3:1-3:

Ephesians 2:4-10:

display

Think through the times you are ready to leave your faith in God to follow another way. Consider your heart in those times: What are you wanting that you don't have now? The answer to this question is crucial for you. It is a time to talk to God, not neglect Him. Tell Him what you want that others offer and remind yourself that, although their ways may sound tempting, you know He has your best interest at heart.

Confess your temptations to God. Talk to Him about what you want out of life. He can handle your grievances. Then ask Him to make you faithful when you are tempted. Thank Him that He cares for you so deeply.

DAY 8

Better Than Money

discover

READ PROVERBS 8.

**For wisdom is better than jewels, and
nothing desirable can equal it.
— Proverbs 8:11**

Many wonder, "What could be better than being rich?" It would be nice to see something you want and be able to purchase it that very minute. Money gives many people a sense of security, power, and prestige. However, Scriptures tells us that "wisdom is better than jewels, and nothing desirable can equal it." Wisdom is better than anything we can desire, even money!

Proverbs 9 goes on to say that wisdom gives wealth to those who love it (see v. 21). It also says that those who listen to wisdom are happy and find life and favor from God (see vv. 34-35). Wealth, happiness, life, and favor from God all come from seeking wisdom. How is this true?

Solomon said the Lord made wisdom at the beginning of creation (see Prov. 8:22). This means before anything was made—including people—God determined what was wise and what was not. When you study the world God made, you find His wisdom. When you shut yourself off from learning, you shut yourself off from wisdom and the wealth, happiness, life, and favor it brings.

delight

Read Psalm 19:1-3. What do these verses teach you about what you can learn from nature?

In you life, how have you found that wisdom is better than money?

display

The great inventor and botanist George Washington Carver said,

> *"To those who have as yet not learned the secret to true happiness, which is the joy of coming into the closest relationship with the Maker and Preserver of all things: begin now to study the little things on your own door yard, going from the known to the nearest related unknown for indeed each new truth brings one nearer to God."* [1]

Spend time outside. Observe your surroundings and talk to God about what you see and have questions about. When you stay curious, you open yourself up to the happiness Carver describes.

---

1 George Washington Carver to Hubert W. Pelt, 24 February 1930, in *George Carver: In His Own Words*, G. R. Kremer, ed., (University of Missouri Press, 1987), 142–143.

Thank God for the wisdom of creation. Ask Him any questions you have about His creation. Also spend some time in quiet observation of God's creation as part of your time with God.

DAY 9

For Your Benefit

discover

READ PROVERBS 9.

"If you are wise, you are wise for your own benefit; if you mock, you alone will bear the consequences."
— Proverbs 9:12

Have you ever played "Marco Polo" in the pool? It's the game where one person, who is supposed to keep his or her eyes closed, calls out "Marco." The other players in the game yell back "Polo." Their voices tell the caller their location and the caller then uses the sound of their voices to determine where they are to tag them. Wisdom is a lot like the game of Marco Polo. Once you start following its voice, you will be able to find it; but if you choose to ignore it, eventually you'll get lost in the deep end.

In Proverbs 9, Solomon talks about who will get wisdom and who won't. It all comes down to how we receive it. When someone gives you instruction, correction, or advice, do you think it over or are you quick to dismiss it? Sometimes we quickly choose not to listen to others, but Solomon warns against this behavior. It only hurts us, not the messenger.

If you consider the message someone is saying to you, regardless of awkward feelings or whether you respect the person or not, wisdom will show itself. Consider the benefits of what following wisdom would be for yourself. If you choose not to consider someone's message out of spite or revenge, you are the one who will suffer the consequences, not that person.

delight

Read 1 Kings 12:3-19, where Rehoboam decided to refuse good advice in favor of following his friends. What were the consequences of his actions?

Think back to a time when you ignored good advice because you didn't like the way it was given to you or the person who gave you the advice. What benefit would you have received if you had simply followed the advice?

display

Next time someone gives you advice, take a moment to think before you respond. Sort out your emotions from the message. If someone made you feel small or inferior and if the situation calls for it, tell them politely, but don't ignore good counsel. Think about what benefits you can receive if you follow the wisdom in what they said. Don't shut out wisdom just because you didn't appreciate how it was given.

Ask God to make you open to hearing wisdom. If someone has hurt your feelings by the way they gave you the advice, talk to God about it. He does care for your feelings, but He doesn't want you to miss out on what is best for you because you were offended.

The Wisdom of Solomon

SECTION 2

When Solomon first became king of Israel, God said He would grant him anything he asked for (see 1 Kings 3:5). Solomon chose wisdom; the ability to know good from evil and to discern what was best for Israel as their king. God was so pleased with this answer, He gave Solomon his request—and anything else he might ever want. What we find in the verses of Proverbs 10–24, is the wisdom God gave Solomon. We would be wise to listen and heed the Word of the Lord.

DAY 10

Living Securely

discover

READ PROVERBS 10.

The one who lives with integrity lives securely, but whoever perverts his ways will be found out.
— Proverbs 10:9

What is "integrity"? As followers of Jesus, integrity is living out the values, morals, and priorities of His kingdom. Living without integrity would be to behave in a way that is opposed to what we value. So let's say someone values honesty but lies. Or people say they value friendship but ghost a close friend when he or she needs help. Those behaviors are examples of not living with integrity.

The greatest role model of integrity that we have is Jesus. He lived in accordance with His values 24/7. He never said or did anything that wasn't in full alignment with His priorities, and yet His life wasn't secure. He was threatened, attacked, betrayed, and killed. So how could Solomon say "the one who lives with integrity lives securely"?

They live securely in the sense that they have no internal turmoil. When we live out what we value, our consciences and our minds can be at ease. It is when we behave in ways not aligned with our values that we are not at peace. Events and circumstances will still be uncertain and tumultuous, but we can have internal rest knowing that when we live out the values God has for us, He'll watch over us.

delight

Think of a time when you acted in a way that wasn't in line with the values you claim as a Christ follower? How did it make you feel?

Jesus gave His harshest rebuke to those who said one thing but acted differently (see Matt. 23:1-7). Why do you think Jesus took such offense to people who behave this way?

display

No one can be like Jesus all the time. There will be times you don't act in alignment with God's values, but the way you react in those times are telling of your true character. If you know you've messed up, fess up. Do whatever you can to right the wrong. God is honored when you live in alignment with His values even when you've messed up before.

Ask God to help you live with integrity. Confess times you behaved out of line. Talk to Him about any values He has that you struggle to live up to.

DAY 11

Words That Harm

discover

READ PROVERBS 11.

A gossip goes around revealing a secret, but a trustworthy person keeps a confidence.
— Proverbs 11:13

Wouldn't it be great if rumors didn't hurt? It'd be so nice if whatever someone said about us had no impact on us. We could just laugh it off, and we'd never think about that piece of gossip again. Logically it seems like words really shouldn't hurt us. They are just words. Why can't the saying "stick and stones will break my bones, but words will never hurt me" be true?

James, the brother of Jesus, said this about our tongues: "The tongue, a world of unrighteousness, is placed among our members. It stains the whole body, sets the course of life on fire" (James 3:6). He compared the tongue to a rudder on a ship and a bit in the mouth of a horse—small objects that determine the whole direction of where they are going (see James 3:3-4). The words we speak will set the direction for our entire lives. They can cause fights, hurt feelings, destroy friendships, and isolate people so much they don't want to live anymore. Whether we want them to or not, our words hold great power.

Gossip is when we use our words to harm others. You may not do it intentionally, but think before you listen to or share things you hear. Ask yourself: "Do I know all the facts? Is sharing this information helping the situation? Would I want this information shared about me?" These questions can guide you into stopping words that could do serious damage to another person's life.

delight

Have you or someone close to you had an experience with hurtful gossip? What did that experience teach you about what you share and who you share it with?

What type of friends do you want to have? Name the characteristics you want most in a friend. Then describe what you need to do to be the kind of friend you want for yourself.

display

Review these questions before passing on information to others: "Do I know all the facts? Is sharing this information helping the situation? Would I want this information shared about me?" If the answer is no to any of these questions, don't spread the information. It is gossip. Decide to be the kind of friend you would want for yourself.

Admit to God that words hold power. Talk to Him about any time someone else's words hurt you. Admit any time you hurt someone else with your words. Ask Him to help you use your words to bless others, not harm them.

DAY 12

Listen to Counsel

discover

READ PROVERBS 12.

A fool's way is right in his own eyes, but whoever listens to counsel is wise.
— Proverbs 12:15

Even the greatest leaders in the world still listen to counsel. In fact, listening to others is part of what makes a great leader. Our president has a Cabinet—a group of fifteen people who oversee various departments and advise the President on how to act. Their advice to the President helps him do his job well. This idea of a Cabinet was considered even as the Constitution was being written. The founding fathers of America knew listening to counsel would enable a President to make wise decisions for our nation.

Many students have a reputation among adults for acting as though they know everything. The danger of refusing to listen to counsel can be costly. When adults give advice, it's because they fear students will make mistakes that can harm their future. Instead of refusing to listen to advice, consider it. Ask the people giving advice why they are giving this advice. What do they fear will happen to you? Ask if they had an experience that influences their advice to you. Then listen. If you consider where they are coming from and their point of view, you may be able to come to a decision that not only helps you but also them.

Proverbs 12:15 doesn't say "the wise person always takes the advice of the counsel" but that he or she listens. Listening to others helps you build great relationships and make informed decisions. As a student, you are under authority and must follow instruction, but as you grow older you will find that goes away. Your everyday decisions become your own, and nobody "makes" you do anything. You get the choice to do your own thing or to be a wise person who listens to godly counsel.

delight

How do you respond to advice?

List some benefits of considering others' points of view when listening to their advice.

display

Think about the people who give you advice. Consider where they are coming from. Ask questions. There is no need to be rude to people who are giving advice even if you disagree. Take time to hear them out, and you can make a more informed decision about your own actions. Decide right now who you keep "butting heads" with and make a list of three questions you can ask them to better understand their point of view.

Talk to God about who gives you counsel. Thank Him for their wisdom. Ask God to help you be discerning when receiving their counsel but also to be open to hear what they want to teach you.

DAY 13

The Company You Keep

discover

READ PROVERBS 13.

**The one who walks with the wise will become wise,
but a companion of fools will suffer harm.
— Proverbs 13:20**

Have you ever done something you regretted just to fit into a group? Dr. Sandra Aamodt says, "adolescents . . . become much more sensitive to peer pressure than they were earlier or will be as adults." This is partly because the brain isn't fully formed until around age twenty-five![2] It's not just your imagination—a strong desire to gain acceptance by a group is in and effects everyone.

Proverbs says the company you keep will greatly influence you. You've probably seen this principle in action. Ever notice yourself talking differently after being around a group of friends—taking on their vocabulary and tone of voice? Did you ever shop for clothes with the purpose of looking more like the group you want to fit in? Proverbs says that this outside influence will go beyond the way you talk and dress to influence your character and future.

It's a shame Solomon didn't listen to his own advice. For political reasons, he married and had relationships with one thousand women (see 1 Kings 11:3). Many were of different religions and swayed him to adopt their gods and abandon his own faith. He let the company he kept steer him from what was most important. God loved Solomon and blessed him with incomparable wisdom and riches, yet Solomon let the people he wanted to impress become priority over the God who gave Him everything.

2 Sandra Aamodt, "Brain Maturity Extends Well Beyond Teen Years," interview by Tony Cox, Tell Me More, NPR, October 10, 2011, https://www.npr.org/templates/story/story.php?storyId=141164708.

delight

Read 1 Kings 11:1-13. What did Solomon do because he wanted to impress his wives instead of God? What were the consequences?

Why do you think it's so hard to resist the pressure to fit in? What are some truths you can tell yourself in moments of temptation?

display

The desire to fit into a group is real. One way to avoid being influenced in negatively is to find a group of friends that will support you to do good. If you are tempted to join a group that will lead you down a path you don't want to take, find a group that is heading in the direction you do want to go. Talk to a trusted adult about where you struggle to find good friends and see if they have suggestions about where you can meet others who will be a good influence on your life.

Thank God for any positive influences in your life. Ask God for help when you are tempted toward foolishness while your friends are around. Talk to God about the direction you want your life to go and ask Him to lead you to the abundant life He has for you.

DAY 14

A Time to Be Wrong

discover

READ PROVERBS 14.

**There is a way that seems right to a person,
but its end is the way to death.
— Proverbs 14:12**

Have you ever heard of an echo chamber? This happens when we seek viewpoints to reinforce what we want to hear while opposing and differing viewpoints are shut out. Echo chambers cause people to become more entrenched in their own beliefs, thoughts, and opinions. They've read and seen enough stories to believe they're right and the opposing side is wrong.[3]

When we stop listening to others, we become closed off to others' thoughts, ideas, and opinions. Along with being honest, upright, and righteous, Proverbs 14 describes the wise as being perceptive, sensible, cautious, and discerning. They seek out knowledge and experiences that will grow their character. In other words, wise people are observant. They are not in their own worlds, closed off to thinking things through. They gather information, dig into topics (not just deciding their opinions after watching a clip online), question from a place of curiosity (not to argue but to understand), and interact with others in person (not just online) to understand how this person behaves in good times and bad.

When we believe that we, and no one else, are the final judges of what is right, we have put ourselves in the place of God. That's a job I don't think you'd want to have. Be wise and allow yourself to learn, have your opinions shaped by truth, and grow in your understanding.

---

3 *The Social Dilemma*, directed by Jeff Orlowski (Boulder, CO: Exposure Labs, 2020), https://www.netflix.com/title/81254224.

delight

Look over the description of the wise person and the foolish person in Proverbs 14. Using the chart below, contrasting the words that describe the wise person and those describing the foolish person. Do you see yourself as responding to others' viewpoints as a fool or a wise person?

WISE	FOOLISH

Think about how you determine right from wrong. Do you only consider your opinion and experiences? What else should you take into consideration when determining if something is a good course of action?

display

Have you spent time researching what you believe? Many people begin to question their faith later in life once they leave their parents or guardians home. Unfortunately, many choose to walk away from faith in Jesus, not because it's untrue, but because they are deceived by teachings that aren't and are pulled away by the allure of the world. A healthy practice at this stage in life is to examine what you believe. We call this owning your faith. Don't just depend on the faith of your family or pastors—see what God's Word says for yourself. Do not be afraid to closely examine what you believe. Read books, talk with trusted mentors, and spend lots of time in God's Word and prayer. Construct a solid faith now based on God's truth and wisdom so that you won't have to deconstruct a flimsy faith later on in life.

Thank God that He is well-suited for His job and that you don't need to have all the answers. Ask for His help as you seek to be open to learning and hearing from Him. Confess times you have thought you were right and might have been rude to someone who was just trying to be helpful.

MEMORY VERSE

A person's heart plans his way, but the Lord determines his steps.

PROVERBS 16:9

DAY 15

Putting Out Fires

discover

READ PROVERBS 15.

A gentle answer turns away anger, but a harsh word stirs up wrath.
— Proverbs 15:1

Have you ever "gotten into it" with someone, meaning you had a huge argument? When an argument gets heated, your physical responses will kick in. Your body will release cortisol and adrenaline—stress hormones that make your heart beat faster—your blood pressure rises, your breathing quickens, and you may find yourself sweating. These bodily sensations can add to your desire to explode in anger against this person immediately.[4]

Just like oxygen feeds a fire, a harsh word raises the temperature of an argument. And just like throwing a wet blanket on a fire kills the flame, a gentle word lowers the temperature. Next time you are in a disagreement, try a gentle word and see what happens. If you do, two things will happen—either the other person will calm down too or they won't and they will look silly arguing with someone who won't fight back with anger and ugly words. It's not easy to do, but with practice you can get better at remaining calm in heated situations.

---

4 "Anger - How It Affects People," Better Health Channel (Department of Health & Human Services, March 30, 2019), https://www.betterhealth.vic.gov.au/health/healthyliving/anger-how-it-affects-people.

delight

Read back through Proverbs 15 and make notes on any reference to your speech. (Words like lips, tongue, word, or answer all refer to speech.) What did you learn? Highlight one of those ideas that can serve as a personal take-away.

Think through your pattern of arguing. Do you try to lower the temperature of the argument or raise it? What are some practical things you can do to make the argument more about coming to a solution and less about attacking the other person?

display

When you can feel your body heating up in an argument, take the following steps: notice that your body is reacting, which may make you feel pressure to attack (verbally or physically), but you don't have to take that route. There is another way. Try slowing down your words and lowering the volume. Try sitting down if you're standing up. If you don't have time to work through the issue at the moment, ask politely if you can discuss this another time when you can think through the issue calmly. Commit to getting to a solution and not to attacking the other person.

Talk to God about why it's difficult for you to use a gentle answer in those times. He cares and wants to help. Thank Him that He will one day make all things right so you can endure when you are hurt by others' anger. Pray for any relationship you have that needs less anger and more gentleness.

DAY 16

He Sees

discover

READ PROVERBS 16.

Commit your activities to the Lord, and your plans will be established.... A person's heart plans his way, but the Lord determines his steps.
— Proverbs 16: 3,9

Have you ever heard someone say, "I feel seen"? It's a statement acknowledging that another person understands you and knows where you are coming from. It feels good to be "seen." Proverbs 16 affirms that God both sees us (knows and gets us) and "sees" us (oversees our whole lives). Even when things go differently from what we expect, He knows us and is with us.

In Genesis 16, Hagar had a child with another woman's husband. She actually lived and worked for this couple. Since the wife (Sarai) couldn't get pregnant, she asked her husband (Abram) to sleep with Hagar. It's a bizarre arrangement. Hagar found herself caring for a child with no help. Her life was hard, but God saw her. He knew her struggle. He cared for her. He came to her and promised her a future for her child. Hagar called God "the one who sees" (Gen. 16:13).

We might think we would like to know our future, but it's better to know who holds the future rather than what the future holds. And the One who holds the future sees and cares for you. He wants good things for you and what He asks of you is to follow His lead through living a life that honors Him. Commit your activities, daily routines, interactions, work, rest, and play to Him. Be faithful with what He has given you today; He will watch over your future. He sees you, always.

delight

Examine your own thoughts about your future. Are you anxious about the future or looking forward to it? Write out your feelings and then look up Psalm 73:23-24. Write this verse below your own thoughts of the future.

What activities do you need to commit to the Lord? Is there something you are doing that may be preventing you from doing God's will?

display

It's so easy to set our minds on the future and what will be. It can be thrilling and exciting, but it can also be worrisome and dreadful. Instead, focus on the present. In each moment, look for how you can be faithful. Ask yourself, "What has God put in front of me to commit to Him?" Maybe it's a skill or a relationship or a habit you need to improve. Name it and dedicate it to God. So what if it's not the skill you do for the rest of your life, a relationship that lasts forever, or a habit that will serve you a year from now? Your faithfulness is seen and honors God right now.

Thank God that He sees you and He holds your future. Ask Him about what He has given you to do now and talk about how to commit your daily activities to Him. Just sit in silence a moment resting in the fact that your God sees and cares for you.

DAY 17

A Friend Like Family

discover

READ PROVERBS 17.

A friend loves at all times, and a brother is born for a difficult time.
— Proverbs 17:17

Friends are a critical component of life for everyone but especially in your teen years. As you begin to find your own identity outside of your parents, you will look for others who will be a part of your support system. In Proverbs 17:17, Solomon advises you to find friends who will love you at all times and become like siblings to you when things get tough. When you find a friend who will be supportive when things are going well and when things are going bad, you have found a bond for life.

Ruth is a great example of a friend to her mother-in-law, Naomi, who was at her lowest point. Naomi's husband had died, and about ten years later, both of her sons died. She was living in an area where she didn't have any other family around—only her daughters-in-law. Naomi felt God was against her and was very depressed. She told Ruth she didn't need to stay with her but to leave and return to her own biological family. Ruth chose to stay with Naomi, though, saying "wherever you go, I will go, and wherever you live, I will live" (Ruth 1:16).

It can be difficult to watch friends suffer. So many times we want to "fix" them. We may even want to tell them what they did wrong and how they could've done things better. But when people are depressed and lonely, they want to know you are like family to them. They want to know you are going to stick around. Just saying, "I care about you, and I'm here for you" can make a world of difference to someone who's suffering.

delight

Think about the role friends play in your own life. How important are they to you? Can you name one act of friendship that made an impact on your life? What was it?

Read Ruth and Naomi's story in Ruth 1:6-17. When you read Ruth's words in verse 16-17, think about someone saying those words to you. What feelings arise in your heart? Why do you think knowing someone will never leave you gives you such a reaction?

display

Do you know someone who needs a loyal friend right now? Maybe you feel inadequate to be that friend, but remember it is not your job to change how someone feels. If someone is depressed, it's not your job to take away their sadness. You are to just be a friend. Think of one thing you can do to let them know you are present for them. Send them a text, meme, or video letting them know they are on your mind. Invite them to hang out. Even if they say no or ghost you, know in your heart you are being a good friend.

Thank God for the friends in your life. If you'd like more or better quality friendships talk to God about your desires. He wants to provide. Ask for His guidance on how to be a good friend to others.

DAY 18

Protection

discover

READ PROVERBS 18.

The name of the Lord is a strong tower; the righteous run to it and are protected.
— Proverbs 18:10

When Solomon compares the name of the Lord to a strong tower he is referring to a tall fortress. Cities built towers so that if they were attacked, the people had a place to go to gather and be protected. They would store food and provisions there so they could outlast their opponents as well. It also provided a place where they could still attack their enemy but be protected at the same time. Additionally the fortress was tall, making it more difficult for the enemy to reach them.

God is like a strong tower that protects and provides in times of turbulence, but who is able to run to Him? Proverbs 18:10 says "the righteous." But who is righteous? (See Rom. 3:10.) In Romans 4:3 the apostle Paul wrote, "Abraham believed God and it was credited to him for righteousness." He was referencing a story that took place in the very beginning of the Bible (see Gen. 15:6). Paul went on to say that all who place their faith in God are credited with righteousness—those who are Abraham's descendants and even those who aren't.

Here is the truth: from the beginning of humanity, it has always been faith in God that brings about righteousness, not perfect obedience to a set of rules. You don't have to do everything right for God to be your strong tower, you must simply trust that He is a strong tower. He will do the providing and the protecting.

delight

Think back on your life. When did you place your faith in God for salvation?

Do you believe God is a strong tower for you? Why or why not?

display

We have established that faith in God is your righteousness, so how do you build your faith? You start by trusting God. The easiest way to do that is through prayer. When something comes up, trust that God wants to help and wants to be involved by talking to Him. Ask for His help. Even if things are perfect at the moment, look for His presence in small ways. Keep coming to Him for help, and He will provide.

Talk to God about your level of trust in Him. Thank Him that you don't have to do everything perfectly to run to Him. Ask Him to build your faith as you continue to revolve your life around Him.

DAY 19

God Takes Out a Loan

discover

READ PROVERBS 19.

Kindness to the poor is a loan to the LORD, and he will give a reward to the lender.
— Proverbs 19:17

Throughout the Bible, you will clearly find that God loves the less fortunate in this world. Over and over again, He instructs those who claim to be His people to care for the poor. God is not unconcerned with people's present situation. Just as He cares for our physical needs, He doesn't want us to ignore the needs of others.

We take out a loan when we want or need to buy something and don't have the funds to pay for it. This means borrowing the funds from someone who does have them and over time paying back the lender (usually with interest). In Proverbs 19:17, the writer said, "Kindness to the poor is a loan to the LORD." This means kindness to the poor is something God wants. He desires to help the poor. He'd love to come in and personally help every needy person, but that is not His divine plan. He has a plan for rescuing the entire world, but He knows for this plan to play out the way He wants, He must wait to make His appearance. In the meantime, He desires for His people to do what He is eagerly awaiting to do in person—care for those in need.

Pause a moment to consider that when you are kind to the poor, you are doing the work of God in such a way that God considers it a loan to Him. How incredible is that? That is great power to have the God of the universe desiring to pay you back for your kindness to the poor. It shows how highly God values the work of helping the poor.

delight

Read Matthew 25:31-46. What do you learn from this passage about how Jesus feels about you helping others in need?

What are the needs Jesus listed in Matthew 25:35-36 in which He felt personally helped? How can you help meet those needs for someone else?

display

There are so many ways to help people in need, but if you are at a loss as to where to begin, start with your local church. If they have any programs that help meet the physical needs of others, ask how you can help. Even if your local church doesn't have a program, they probably support other organizations that do and can connect you with them. Also, be observant to the needs of those around you. Jesus mentioned welcoming a stranger as a way to show kindness to Him, so when you see people being left out, try including them.

Thank God that He not only cares about the spiritual needs of others but also the physical. Ask Him to help you see ways that you can show kindness to those in need.

DAY 20

The Privilege of Work

discover

READ PROVERBS 20.

**The slacker does not plow during planting season;
at harvest time he looks, and there is nothing.
— Proverbs 20:4**

Did you realize that even before sin entered the world God gave humans work to do? Yes, God designed work for us; work did not come about from sin (see Gen. 2:15). There are many benefits to work. Through work we are able to provide for ourselves and others, it gives us challenges in life, and it can open us up to new things. Without work we would all suffer from hunger and from lack of innovation and entertainment. We wouldn't want to live in a world without work.

Throughout Proverbs, you have probably noticed that hard work is commended. (See Prov. 12:11,24; 13:4; 14:23; 20:4; 21:5; and 22:29). In contrast, laziness is described as leading to poverty and hunger. (See Prov. 19:15,24; 20:13). It may seem like these teachings are obvious, right, and fair—if you work you become prosperous, and if you don't, you won't. But there are times when someone who didn't work hard will be rewarded and those who did work hard will be overlooked. How do we handle the wisdom of this Proverb and what we see out in the world?

Colossians 3:23-24 says, "Whatever you do, do it from the heart, as something done for the Lord and not for people, knowing that you will receive the reward of an inheritance from the Lord. You serve the Lord Christ." The work you do can not only enrich your life here on earth but will also enrich your eternal life with God. He has an inheritance for you!

delight

How do you see work? Do you think of it as a blessing or a pain? How can knowing that God designed you to work help give you a more positive view of work?

Name some earthly and eternal benefits of work.

display

It's very likely you view work as something you don't want to do or try to put off. Try reframing your thinking. Look at the work in front of you as to your benefit and to God's. There will always be things that need to get done—homework needs to be done, yards need to be mowed, and belongings will need to be returned to their proper place. These jobs don't exist to irritate you but to help you learn habits that will go toward a fulfilling life. They are also jobs that help you and the people you live with thrive.

Thank God for the work He has given you to do. Confess times you have not been grateful for work. Ask for His help to see work as a benefit to you and a chance to honor Him.

DAY 21

The Gifts God Accepts

discover

READ PROVERBS 21.

Doing what is righteous and just is more acceptable to the Lord than sacrifice.
— Proverbs 21:3

I am the kind of person who likes knowing exactly what I am getting on my birthday and Christmas. I do not appreciate surprises, so I make out lists of gift suggestions for family members. I like to shop for myself, and when it is time to treat myself with a present, I already have in mind what I want. In Proverbs 21:3, God tells us exactly the kind of gifts He wants to receive. No guessing on our part. God knows what He wants, and He doesn't hold back in telling us.

God finds doing what is right and just more acceptable than any possession or amount of money you have. He is much more concerned with how you live than with what you can offer. Remember, God made the world, so there is not really any possession on earth that God would desire. Instead, He wants more than anything for His people to live lives that honor Him.

God wants your obedience to Him—living out the commands He has for you. Jesus said, "If you continue in my word, you really are my disciples" (John 8:31). It doesn't mean you do everything right all the time. It does mean examining your life to make sure your desire is to live out what God values, working through conflicts with others, and being honest with God when you see an area where you need help. That kind of attitude is what God wants more than any gift you could offer Him.

delight

Look up 1 Samuel 15:22; Psalm 51:16-17; Isaiah 1:11-17; Hosea 6:6; and Matthew 5:23-24. From these verses, what does God desire more than sacrifices?

Have you ever had the experience where someone gave you a gift or did you a favor, but it felt more like they wanted something from you in return? How did that make you feel? How did it affect your relationship with that person?

display

Have you mistaken some external object as something God desires more than an your obedience to Him? Think about it—do you think God is concerned with how much time you go to church or read your Bible if you are still treating others poorly and being selfish? Or have you tried to manipulate God by promising you'll do certain things but continue to live in disobedience to Him? Let Proverbs 21:3 be your wake-up call. God isn't interested in any behavior or offering you give if your heart is not in a place of willingness to obey Him.

Examine your motives for living the Christian life. Is your heart in the right place? Talk to God about it. Then consider what it would mean to do what is right and just in your current situation.

DAY 22

Habit Becomes Destiny

discover

READ PROVERBS 22.

Start a youth out on his way; even when he grows old he will not depart from it.
— Proverbs 22:6

Is there something you do every day without noticing you are doing it? Maybe you put on your seatbelt on as soon as you get in the car. Or you always check your phone as soon as school ends. We all have habits that we do without paying attention. Scientists have found that when we first start a new behavior, neurons in our brain fire in a sequence, but when that sequence becomes repetitive, neurons only fire at the beginning and end of the sequence. In other words, the longer we do something, the more on "autopilot" our brains become.[5]

Proverbs 22:6 is a principle: when a young person starts out on the right path, as he grows, he will stay on that path. This means creating good habits now sets you on a good path for years to come. It's easier to create those "autopilot" habits when you are young than to try to learn them when you are older.

Decide now what path you'd like to be on so you can practice the habits that will get you there. If you practice habits that will yield great spiritual reward, this will set you up for a rewarding life for years to come.

---

5 Maria Chute, "What Happens in the Brain When Habits Form?," Medical News Today (MediLexicon International, February 11, 2018), https://www.medicalnewstoday.com/articles/320874#Brain-patterns-that-indicate-habits.

delight

What habits have shaped your life to this point? Have they been good habits that set you on a good path or not? Explain.

What are some habits that are essential for people to grow in their faith?

display

Think about the kind of life that pleases God. What characteristics does that person possess? (If you have no idea, you can start by looking up Galatians 5:22-23.) Now consider the habits that help you get to that life. List habits you'd like to develop, and then list habits you probably need to change. Keep those lists close for reference, but pick only one habit to either develop or eliminate. Remember, lasting change happens when we take small steps with consistency.

Discuss the direction of your life with God. Do you like where it is headed? Do you think He wants something different for you? Talk about habits that you know you need to work on and habits you need to stop. Seek His guidance as you seek to honor Him with your life.

DAY 23

Parents Matter

discover

READ PROVERBS 23.

Listen to your father who gave you life, and don't despise your mother when she is old.
— Proverbs 23:22

God puts great importance on parents and the respect children should show them. Among the ten commandments, the only one with a promise attached to it is the command to "honor your father and mother" (Ex. 20:12). And what is that promise? "That you may have a long life in the land that the LORD your God is giving you" (Ex. 20:12). God designed parents to have a deep concern and love for their children. Their instructions to you are for your good.

Listening to your parents, guardians, or whomever is raising you is important to God. He chose for you to be in their family, whether through birth, circumstance, or adoption. He designed the family to be a support system. Parents support their children by providing them a home, clothing, and nourishment. Your parents probably also give you many more things like—their wisdom, time, and affection. Make no mistake, your parents aren't perfect, but they care for you.

God wants you to honor your parents by listening to them and not disregarding their words. It doesn't mean they are always right and you can't have an opinion. It simply means you are to consider what they say and be respectful when you reply back. It honors God when you show honor to your parents.

delight

Do you see your parents (or parental figure) as important as God tells us they are? Why or why not?

What role do your parents play in supporting you?

display

Studies have shown that positive communication about beliefs, feelings, and experiences shared between parents and children protects you from health risks and helps you do better in school.[6] Your parents may very well be wrong about some things but engaging in respectful conversation with them will benefit you. So next time they offer their unsolicited advice, take a deep breath. Respond with courtesy and a willingness to hear them out.

---

6 "Increase the Proportion of Children and Adolescents Who Communicate Positively with Their Parents - EMC-01," Increase the proportion of children and adolescents who communicate positively with their parents - EMC-01 - Healthy People 2030, accessed December 21, 2022, https://health.gov/healthypeople/objectives-and-data/browse-objectives/children/increase-proportion-children-and-adolescents-who-communicate-positively-their-parents-emc-01.

Thank God for your parents or whoever is standing in the place of your parents at the moment. If you need more patience or kindness in your interactions with them, ask God for it.

DAY 24

Envy and Jealousy

discover

READ PROVERBS 24.

Don't envy the evil or desire to be with them, for their hearts plan violence, and their words stir up trouble.
— Proverbs 24:1-2

Have you ever found yourself wanting what someone else has, even if that person is not the kind of person you want to be? You are not alone in this feeling. In Psalm 73, the psalmist sympathizes with these feelings. He saw the wicked living the easy life. They were healthy, wealthy, and fed, and people were flocking to be in their presence. It was nauseating for the psalmist to witness. They totally ignored God and yet their lives seemed perfect. It just didn't seem fair. What's the point in doing good when the evil prosper?

In Proverbs 24, Solomon warns every wise person not to envy the wicked. That's easier said than done when the wicked are prospering. When someone else's life looks so much better than ours, the temptation to compromise who we are weighs heavily on us. What can we do? The psalmist gives his solution: he went to God's sanctuary and reminded himself of how good God was to him (see vv. 16-17,25-28). Now don't discount this solution if it seems too simplistic.

Your belief in God changes everything about what you value. If you believe God rewards those who live for Him, then there is no need to worry about the prosperity of the wicked because the One you serve is greater than money and affluence. God is not unsympathetic to your feelings though—that's why He has left promise after promise in the Bible that He sees you, He cares for you, and He will reward your faithfulness.

delight

Look up these Scriptures and name the promises of God in each one.

   A. Psalm 34:18

   B. Matthew 5:3-12

   C. John 10:7-10 (sheep are a metaphor for God's people)

   D. Philippians 3:18-21

display

If you struggle with envy, it is time to take God seriously at His word. Talk to Him about what He has promised you and how you feel. Cling to Him. Refer to the promises in His Word and ask Him to remind you of His presence. It will also help to find people who are walking alongside you in your faith. They are part of God's gift to you as you seek to remove envy and live for God's glory.

Talk to God about envy that is living in your heart. It doesn't do any good to ignore it. God knows it's there. He wants to work with you on looking to Him to fulfill your desires and not to entertain the way of the wicked.

Wisdom that Endures

SECTION 3

Believe it or not, one day you will be old. It will be you needing a young person to show you how to update your phone or log onto a streaming service rather than the other way around. Even many of the things you know how to do now will no longer be needed in the years to come. Don't believe me? Ask your parents about VCRs. But wisdom will never stop being important. In the final section of Proverbs, God's Word reveals wisdom that endures; wisdom greater than the here today and gone tomorrow obsessions of our time.

DAY 25

Dealing with Enemies

discover

READ PROVERBS 25.

If your enemy is hungry, give him food to eat, and if he is thirsty, give him water to drink, for you will heap burning coals on his head, and the LORD will reward you.
— Proverbs 25:21-22

Every single one of us has been wronged by someone before. Whether by people talking behind our backs or lying to our faces or any number of other scenarios, we all know what it feels like to be wronged. When we're wronged, we often want to pay back the person who hurt us so that they might feel the same pain we felt. This feeling is called revenge. We have this feeling because God created us with a desire for justice.

But our idea of revenge isn't God's justice. The Bible teaches that vengeance belongs to God and God alone. Jesus even went so far as to say we should love our enemies and pray for those who persecute us (see Matt. 5:44). The apostle Paul quoted Proverbs 25:21-22 in his letter to the Romans (see 12:20). Does this mean following Jesus requires giving up on justice? Not at all. What these verses tell us is that Jesus reframes our understanding of justice. Thanks to Jesus, we don't have to get even with our enemies.

Ultimately, our greatest enemies are not people but sin and death. Jesus has defeated these enemies through His death and resurrection. So, how do we participate in God's work of establishing justice on earth? It may seem strange, but we do so by loving, feeding, and serving the very people who seem to be against us.

delight

Be honest with yourself: who in your life do you tend to think of as an enemy? Why?

Have you ever tried serving this person or showing him or her kindness in some way? If not, what is holding you back?

What is one small way you could serve or show kindness to someone you've been at odds with lately?

display

The idea of loving your enemies probably seems pretty tough. The longer you have been at odds with someone the harder it is to imagine being kind to them or serving them. There is always the chance that if you did show some kindness to your enemies they might spit in your face (literally or figuratively). If you want to participate in Jesus's mission of bringing justice to earth, consider starting small. If you've been at odds with another player on your soccer team, you don't have to bake her or him cookies. Maybe just start by saying "hi" next time you see them at practice. You might be surprised by how small gestures of kindness could lead to greater opportunities for ministry.

Thank God for loving you even though, because of your sin, you were once His enemy. Ask Him to help you join His work of establishing justice by showing kindness and love to both your neighbors and enemies. Pray for an "enemy" by name, asking God to give you the courage necessary to show this person kindness, love, and respect.

DAY 26

Drop the Mask

discover

READ PROVERBS 26.

A hateful person disguises himself with his speech and harbors deceit within.
— Proverbs 26:24

Have you ever been to a Comic-Con or seen the elaborate costumes people wear to look like their favorite super heroes or comic book characters? The term for this is cosplay, and there are some truly amazing artists who are so skilled that, if you didn't know better, you might actually think the person is Capitan America or Wonder Woman.

You may never have done cosplay or worn an elaborate costume at Halloween, but chances are, you have experience at crafting disguises. As human beings broken by sin, we all have a tendency to hide who we truly are from the people around us. We don't literally wear costumes, but we downplay our weaknesses and talk up our strengths. We brag about our biggest accomplishments and most interesting experiences on social media while never mentioning our frustrations, insecurities, or failures. Following Jesus doesn't require confessing all our sins and failures on social media, but the gospel is an invitation to authenticity. Because Jesus died for our sins and rose to offer us new life, we can stop trying to pretend we're someone else. The gospel reminds us that God loves us and accepts us through Jesus and not because we are good or important.

Proverbs 26:24 reminds us that deceiving ourselves and others harms us and them. It is time to drop whatever masks we've been wearing and embrace the identity we've been given in Christ as children of God. If we'll drop our masks, we'll be happier and better positioned to love and serve the people around us.

delight

Ask yourself, "What mask or masks am I wearing right now? How am I trying to deceive others?"

How might your life be different if you stopped trying to pretend you are better or more popular or more important than others?

How can pretending to be someone you are not cause harm to other people? How will you fight the temptation to do so this week?

display

Find a notebook or journal and make a list of times recently you were tempted to pretend to be better at something or more knowledgeable about a subject than you are. Then make a list of things you know about yourself because of Jesus. (For example: I know God loves me, I know I am a child of God, I know my sin is forgiven, etc.). Thank God that who you are in Christ is so much better than you who you've pretended to be.

Ask God to give you the courage to stop pretending to be someone you are not. Pray that through Jesus, He would free you from always feeling like you need to compete with other people to prove your worth. Thank God that you are loved, accepted, and have a meaningful purpose.

memory verse

Proverbs 25:21-22

If your enemy is hungry, give him food to eat, and if he is thirsty, give him water to drink, for you will heap burning coals on his head, and the Lord will reward you.

DAY 27

No One Is an Island

discover

READ PROVERBS 27.

Iron sharpens iron, and one person sharpens another.
— Proverbs 27:17

Sometimes I don't want anyone else's help or guidance. Sometimes I want to do things on my own. If you are honest with yourself, you probably sometimes feel the same way. When you were younger, you probably got annoyed when a parent or an older sibling poured your cereal because you knew you were capable of doing it yourself. As you got older, there came a point when you no longer wanted your parent or caretaker to walk you to the bus stop. Now you find it annoying when your parents don't let you go places by yourself or monitor your activities on your phone or computer.

We feel this way because our sin nature would have us believe that we are bigger, smarter, better, and more important than we actually are. Because of this we all have a tendency to inflate our importance and contribution and downplay that of others. This mentality harms us and our neighbors because God never intended for us to make it on our own. We were made for community.

Proverbs 27:17 tells us that God has strategically placed people in our lives to help us grow and thrive. The same is true of us and our relationships with others. God wants to use your strengths and experiences to bless and serve the people around you. The invitation to follow Jesus is an invitation to life-giving relationships that will help you grow in ways you never would have thought possible.

delight

What is one way you could "sharpen" a friend, neighbor, or teammate this week?

When was a time in your life when someone sharpened you? When was a time when you sharpened someone else?

display

Who sets a good example of what it means to follow Jesus? What is one practical way you could seek "sharpening" from that person? Journal one way you could be an encouragement to a friend or neighbor this week. Additionally journal about one person you'd like to learn more from and one way you could learn from the good example that person sets when it comes to following Jesus.

Thank God for the gift of community. Praise Him for putting people in your life to help you grow and give you a good example of what it looks like to follow Jesus. Ask God to help you set a good example for the people around you and to give you a heart to help others grow and thrive in their walk with Jesus.

DAY 28

More than Money

discover

READ PROVERBS 28.

Better the poor person who lives with integrity than the rich one who distorts right and wrong.
— Proverbs 28:6

We live in a culture that cares a lot about money. Pop stars are always singing or rapping about it. TV shows glorify people trying to get more of it and even doing really awful things to get rich. If we're honest, we probably dream about having a lot of money one day so that we can go on elaborate vacations and own big houses or fancy cars. Because so much of what we do requires money, it is easy to think money is more important than it actually is, at least in terms of God's kingdom.

Proverbs 28:6 looks forward to the kinds of things Jesus would teach about money and blessing. For example Jesus opened the Sermon on the Mount by declaring, "Blessed are the poor in spirit" (Matt. 5:3). And another time Jesus met a rich young ruler who wanted to know how he could have eternal life, and Jesus told him to sell all that he had and give to the poor (see Matt. 19:16-22).

This doesn't mean money doesn't matter and you should also sell all that you own. Instead, Proverbs 28:6 and Jesus's teaching on money tell us that money isn't nearly as important as we tend to think it is. Following Jesus reframes how we view whatever money or assets we possess. Rather than seeing these things solely as means of providing for yourself or getting ahead, Jesus opens our eyes to how these things can be tools for His kingdom.

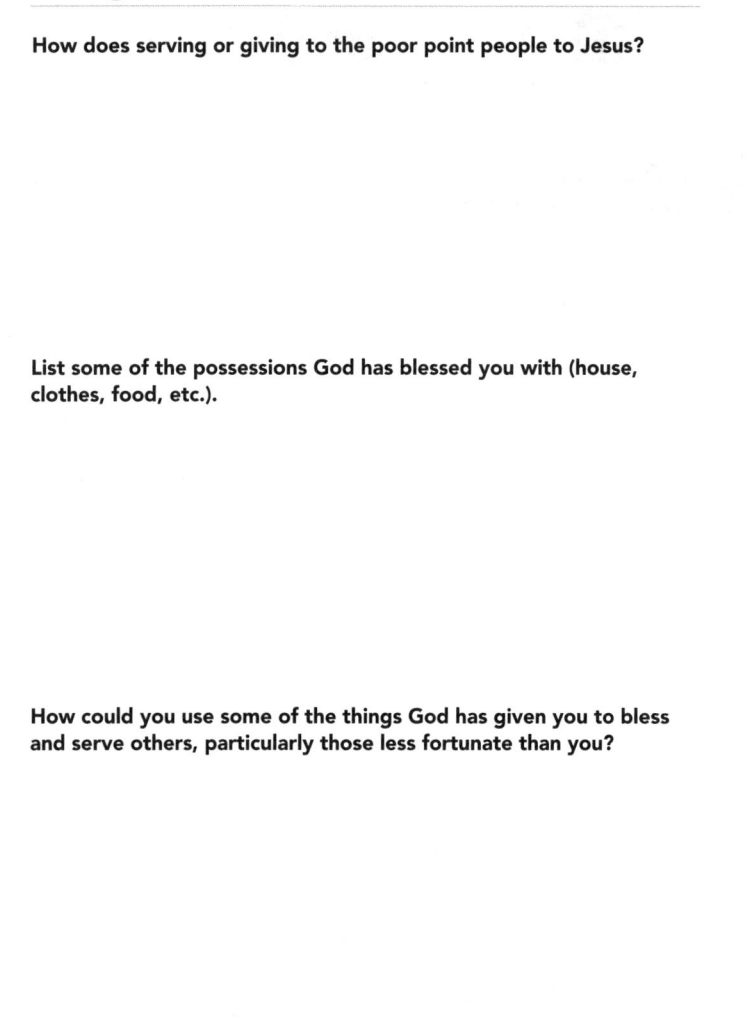

delight

How does serving or giving to the poor point people to Jesus?

List some of the possessions God has blessed you with (house, clothes, food, etc.).

How could you use some of the things God has given you to bless and serve others, particularly those less fortunate than you?

display

We live in a culture that is obsessed with stuff. It seems like there is never a time when we are not being advertised some new product that will supposedly make our lives better. Journal your response to the following question: How should followers of Jesus have a different attitude about money and possessions?

Thank God that through Jesus, you can be freed from slavery to money and possessions. Ask Him to help you live like He is King and a relationship with Him is far better than all the money in the world. Ask Him to open your eyes to ways you could use your money or possessions to serve Him and your neighbors.

DAY 29

The Way to Happiness

discover

READ PROVERBS 29.

Without revelation people run wild, but one who follows divine instruction will be happy.
— Proverbs 29:18

What rule at home or at school drives you nuts? Maybe it is your curfew? You might ask, "Why won't my parents trust me to stay out later?" Or maybe it is having to sit still at school, and you think, "If am done with my work, why do I have stay seated at my desk?" It is easy to think we know better than other people, but maybe if we slowed down, we might think of some reasons such rules are in place. We might even see that these rules are designed for our good and the good of others—to protect us and our neighbors.

"Revelation" in verse 18 does not refer to future-telling prophecies but rather to the words or instruction from God. In other words, this verse is telling us to pay attention to and follow God's rules, guidance, and instruction. Even though rules often feel restrictive to us, they are typically rooted in a good purpose. This is far more true of God's teaching than any human rules. Revelation is designed to give us wisdom, to help us grow and join in God's kingdom work. In fact, according to verse 18, God intends for His rules to make us happy. So instead of seeing the teaching of God's Word as holding us back, we should see it as something that pushes us forward into life and joy and into the mission God has given us.

delight

According to Proverbs 29:18, what do people tend to do when they ignore God's instructions? Why is that?

How does the teaching of the Bible give your direction? Joy?

display

What is one step you could take this week to make time for studying the Bible and considering God's teaching? Make a plan to get into the Bible more consistently this week. Jot down your plan. How will you make time for Bible study? When will you read the Bible? How will you make sure you don't just read it but put into practice? Outline a plan and share it with a friend or mentor who will hold you accountable to follow through.

Thank God for how He gives us life and joy through His Word. Ask Him to help you trust that His teachings are good and true.

DAY 30

Stay True to the Word

discover

READ PROVERBS 30-31.

Every word of God is pure; he is a shield to those who take refuge in him. Don't add to his words, or he will rebuke you, and you will be proved a liar.
— Proverbs 30:5-6

Have you ever twisted or reframed something a parent or guardian said to try to get around it? Maybe they told you it was time to take a break from video games but you reinterpreted them to mean, "Get off as soon as you finish the level or round." Or maybe they said, "You can't watch that movie," and you interpreted that as, "You can't watch that movie at our house." So you watched it at your friend's house instead. This is the kind of thing the writer of Proverbs is warning against in verse 6, only with much higher stakes because He is talking about God's words.

We all have a desire to twist teaching or commands to mean something they don't so that we can feel free to do what we want to do. The problem with doing this, however, is the outcome outlined in verse 6, "[God] will rebuke you, and you will be proved a liar."

The point of these verses is bigger than warning us not to try and trick God. The writer of these proverbs wants us to know God's words are good, empowering, and protecting. More than just keeping us in line, God's Word unlocks wisdom, our potential, gives us hope, and protects us from harm that can come our way.

delight

What do these verses tell us about the power of God's teaching? Why is it such a big deal to add to God's Word?

When is a time you have taken refuge in God and His Word?

display

Did you formulate a plan to get into the Bible (see Day 29)? Have you implemented any of that plan yet? If not, what is holding you back. Did you ask for a friend to hold you accountable to doing so? Contact that friend today and give her or him an update.

Thank God that His Word gives you life and protects you. Ask Him to help you trust that He is at work guiding you. Ask Him to help you live out the teaching and wisdom of Proverbs this week.

W-I-S-D-O-M

Sometimes wisdom feels like something that comes only with age or only to specific people. We do gain wisdom as we grow up, but wisdom isn't all about how old you are or your personality—wisdom is about having a heart and mind open to God. God wants to give "generously and ungrudgingly" to those who seek wisdom (James 1:5). Whether you're thirteen or eighteen or thirty or eighty, or whether you're serious or shy or goofy or outgoing—wisdom is for you.

Wisdom isn't just for our benefit, though; it brings God glory and helps us love others too. Throughout this devotional, we've studied wise practices and ways to grow in wisdom. So, use the following acronym to identify practical and specific ways you can continue to seek wisdom that comes from above (see James 3:17-18).

W-Word

Be in God's Word.

What are you studying in God's Word right now?

What has God been teaching you through His Word lately?

Name one piece of wisdom you've learned from studying God's Word over the last month.

I-Imitator

Be an imitator. Imitate Jesus and other godly leaders.

Who are you imitating?

How does your life show it?

Who are some godly people you can imitate?

S-Seeker

Be a seeker. Seek God in prayer and seek the lost.

What are you seeking God for right now?

Write out your heart's prayer or your deepest need this week.

Who do you know who doesn't know Jesus? How can you help these people see who Jesus is, what He has done for them, how He loves them, and how He changes our lives for the better?